# Gift from the Garden

Trellis Publishing, Inc.
P.O. Box 280
New York Mills, MN 56567

For information about special discounts for bulk purchases or for a book club question list, please contact Trellis Publishing special sales at 1-800-513-0115
Printed in China

3 5 7 9 10 8 6 4 2

Publisher's Cataloging-in-Publication
(Provided by Quality Books, Inc.)

    DuBois, Bernie, author.
       Gift from the garden / by Bernie DuBois.
       pages cm
       LCCN 2016916665
       ISBN 978-1-930650-26-8 (hardcover)
       ISBN 978-1-930650-27-5 (ebook)

       1. Life.  2. Life cycle, Human.    I. Title.

    BD435.D815 2017         128
               QBI16-900059

Cover Design by Mitch Blessing, Bemidji, Minnesota
Interior Design by Gary Kruchowski, Duluth, Minnesota

# Gift from the Garden

By
Bernie DuBois

# Contents

# Introduction

If you've ever read the classic, *Gift from the Sea* you'll know what inspired this book. I'll always remember when I found that little book, in which Anne Morrow Lindbergh described her life and compared the lives of women to various sea shells. It may sound strange, but her book was truly a gift to help me realize that we all go through stages and that life carries on, ever in pace with the currents, the tides, and the life of the sea.

My garden and the even more spectacular gardens of others help me stay calm and realize that the earth is a healing place, that where there is green there is hope, and that failure (or better put, a lack of success) is only temporary because each spring there is indeed a new beginning. Move a plant here, trim a tree there, and we have a different view of the world. We can become like our gardens – renewing and redefining ourselves, every year starting a fresh cycle of our lives.

# Dedication

To my mother, whose voice I could remember during this
writing. I can picture the back of her legs, which by the end of
the summer were always darker in the back than in the front,
because she wore shorts and spent so many hours on her knees in
her garden.

# Acknowledgements

My thanks go out to the many people who helped make this book
possible, and who have supported me throughout this process.
To my sisters, who are my constant source of comfort, insight,
and fun – thank you for your help with this book and with my
life. To Liz and Toby, who edit my words. To Mitch, who creates
such beautiful book covers that it's impossible to choose between
them. To my friends and colleagues who help create all of these
rich life experiences I have to write about. To Lindy, who gives
up time that we can spend together, and to his support of my
endless endeavors. And to my agent, Georg Karlov, who always
encourages my creative side.

# Weeds

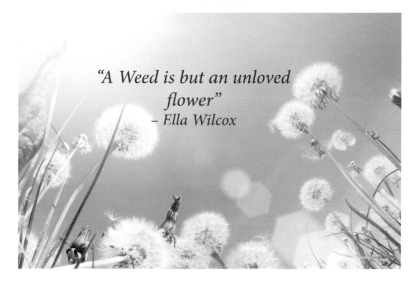

> "A Weed is but an unloved flower"
> – Ella Wilcox

We may as well start with weeds, since they take up so much of our time and attention. Right now my garden is being invaded by quack grass around the edges – grass that was purposefully let grow to anchor the surrounding soil so the whole thing, which is perched on a hillside, would not slide into a neighboring slough hole. That grass, once carefully tended and intentionally valued, is now a weed. I want it gone! It chokes my irises and messes up my lilies, not to mention that it just looks sloppy. Sometimes being a weed is temporary; after all, the definition of a weed is a plant that is growing where it is not wanted. The most beautiful of maple trees would be considered a weed in a potato field. And almost every plant is scowled upon at a building site being prepared for new construction. Once the bulldozer begins clearing, every plant is a pesky weed!

Have you ever looked around and realized you do not fit in with all the people around you? How can we possibly feel like we fit in everywhere? Of course that is not possible. Perhaps for you it is just a fleeting moment or a few moments while you get your bearings in a group. You might feel that you are either in the wrong room, or wearing the wrong clothes, or dancing in uncomfortable shoes, or your hair just isn't quite right. You feel like a weed among gardenias.

Or maybe you live in a place where you just don't fit in. You've always loved the bustle of the city, but you are living in a small rural area where everyone knows you. So you go through your days longing for a cup of city cappuccino coffee or a stroll on the busiest of streets. Or you are most comfortable among rows of corn, and instead you live in a loft in New York or Los Angeles, fighting traffic, longing for the sweet smell of cow manure or the sight of corn ripening in the fields.

Being a weed can make you paranoid. After all, folks are out there with weed killers! Herbicides! Spray units! Even a role that you play in your life can feel foreign – such as being a new mom, or being a stay-at-home mom, or being a working mom – and no matter what your choices, there might be moments when your role just doesn't feel natural. Like the song says, ". . . a lonely little petunia in an onion patch . . ."

Relax. You may fit in eventually – or perhaps with time your rocky ground might become fertile enough to be considered home.

I have been a weed many times. One of the first times was during my first quarter as a student at the local community college, when somehow as a child, I had gotten the idea that the only people meant to succeed in college are the brainiacs. But there I was, at the age of 27, going back to school with all those young college students who seemed like they could breeze through any exam. Looking back on it now, I wonder why I felt old and out of place, because now nearly half the classroom in a community college is made up of nontraditional-age students – those who have been out of high school at least five years – along with some students who are retirement age. My very first test was in sociology, and I received a D. Wake up call! I had to learn what the teacher wanted on the tests, learn to study harder, buckle down, and prove to myself that I was not a weed and that I belonged in college. And the same thing happened to me when I transferred to a four-year university. Talk about feeling out of place!

It's easy to feel out of place when you get a new job as well. I've often wondered when my new employer might discover that they have hired the wrong person – there is no way that I know how to teach this course, or run this college, or handle these projects. But eventually I would learn what was necessary, buckle down, and prove to myself that I was up for whatever challenges that came my way. My weed status would eventually change to at least a pleasant border ground cover, if not a show plant: sturdy, useful.

Even as a new mom, I remember wondering how other people seemed to nurture automatically, or if somehow other women had built-in momma genes that I didn't have. Weed in a momma patch – especially since I had already tasted the freedom of feminism yet was living in a rural, traditional place on the Iron Range of Minnesota: Democratic in politics but conservative about women's roles. I learned from the other women around me, gifted with some of their caring and advice, and eventually my momma roots took hold, and my children turned out great – the ultimate proof that we can grow into those roles that at first seem insurmountable, and we can become accustomed to those places where we don't quite fit in.

It can work the other way as well. It might be that once you felt welcome but not so anymore. You might have been accepted at one time, and now you are feeling like a stranger either in your own home or at your workplace. Perhaps your ideas or philosophies have moved past those whose company you keep.

Don't despair. You might be just what is needed to keep the whole operation – be it family, workplace or community project – from falling into the slough hole!

# *Roses*

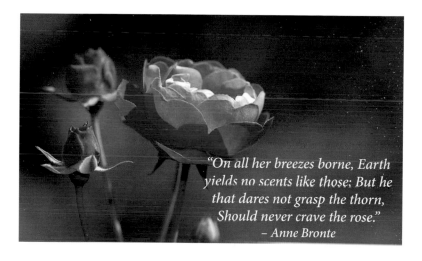

*"On all her breezes borne, Earth
yields no scents like those; But he
that dares not grasp the thorn,
Should never crave the rose."*
*– Anne Bronte*

Roses are gorgeous plants and give us colorful blooms and rose hips for medicinal purposes. The varieties are limitless and range from the smallest tea rose to fences of climbing roses that can serve as hedges.

My roses need the most care of all my plants. From the first buds of spring and the pruning of old winter growth, to making sure they get enough water during the summer months, to protecting them over the winter with some kind of shelter, they take constant attention. I prune mine so that the wind takes care of most of the pests, and I make sure that they get at least a bucket full of water a week. They need to be fertilized and watched carefully for any sign of disease. I love being able to cut a rose or two for the kitchen table during the summer, and to me, that is well worth the effort of their care. Even wild rose bushes have a beauty that makes one "stop and smell the roses."

Have you ever walked into the room and felt like the most beautiful creature that walked the earth? I think of celebrities on the red carpet that must get a sense of their beauty reflected back at them through admiration and grateful crowds. Oh, but the heavy price that one pays to be a rose.

It can be difficult to be around such beauty, especially when that person has come to rely on admiration. Those thorns! People who come to expect admiration can get prickly if you don't notice them or pay them the compliments they expect. And it can hurt to be near them if they take your friendship or your love for granted.

I'm reminded of a friend of mine who never has a hair out of place, her home is always in order and her children seem impeccably clean and well-mannered. I get exhausted just watching her get ready to go somewhere. Even the jewelry must match the outfit, which must match the place we are going, which must match the mood. And of course I can never live up to the expectation to do the same.

If you want to be a rose, prepare to spend your life in an effort to always keep up that beauty. Some do it very successfully, especially those in the public eye and who have the resources to carry it off. They go to the gym regularly, eat right, and they probably have never gone to bed without doing their face-cleansing ritual. And some do it seemingly effortlessly, like Cindy Crawford. She seems to look gorgeous even when the camera catches her unaware. Maybe you are a rose, and you get great joy out of looking just right for any occasion. You have perhaps always turned heads, and it can be a powerful feeling.

I remember once feeling as though I was stunning. It was prom night, my junior year in high school. Maybe it was because my mother had sewn me a white satin jacket, and I wore a teal-colored long dress with matching shoes purchased for my older sister's wedding. So for a family without many resources, I felt like a princess. I even spent the money to get my hair done at the beauty parlor (which is what we called them in those days). It was an updo with big curls – probably the first and only time I had "big hair." And gloves! Ah, for the days of long white gloves! Many people told me that night that I looked beautiful, but what mattered most was that I felt beautiful. Never before nor since have I used that word when describing myself.

Have you had your rose moment? It's never too late to give that a whirl. Or are you an exhausted rose? Beauty changes as we age, and there are so many examples of gorgeous women of experience. Sophia Loren never lost her luster. Take a look at her in the movie "Nine," singing Guarda la Luna at the age of 75, and you'll long for the attributes of a rose. Audrey Hepburn is another example, but because of her death at age 63, we never will get to see her in old age; yet clearly she was aging beautifully and she represented her causes (UNICEF and others) with great grace and style.

Do you have such roses in your family or community? I know many who brighten my day just by seeing them. And although the adage is true that beauty is only skin deep and it is far more important to be a beautiful person on the inside, there's no crime in enjoying beauty in its many physical forms, and I appreciate those people who try and look their best. My mother-in-law asked that at her funeral, would the men in the family please wear white dress shirts. Almost all of them did. She wanted the men to look their best on that day of her formal laying to rest, and to her, that meant men in white shirts.

No, I'm no rose. I'm lucky if I remember to comb my hair on my way out the door. I once had the nickname "rat's nest Mary" because there was no getting a comb through the back of my hair – that is how unrose-like I was as a little girl, and I still carry that love of getting totally dirty and unkempt. Still, I hope that you've had a rose moment, and that you lived in and enjoyed that moment. And if not, why not make one now? Do whatever makes you feel beautiful, or special, or appreciated, even if it is just for yourself. A luxurious pampering bath, a special skin cream, or a night on the town can make you feel rosy.

# *Annuals*

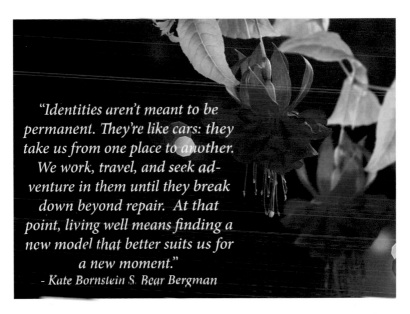

"Identities aren't meant to be permanent. They're like cars: they take us from one place to another. We work, travel, and seek adventure in them until they break down beyond repair. At that point, living well means finding a new model that better suits us for a new moment."
- Kate Bornstein S. Bear Bergman

There's nothing like annuals to add variety to your garden and surroundings. You can choose any color, any height, any multiple features such as light leaves or dark; short, squat plants versus tall beauties; delicate blooms or showiness that almost makes you look away, embarrassed for them and their brassiness.

Half-grown girls remind me of annuals. They have yet to conform, and they are willing to try out their own style – be it goth or elegant, casual or dress-up. They have not yet restricted themselves to one way of looking at the world.

In a garden full of garish annuals, I don't even know where to look. Yet where would we be without those easy-to-grow splashes of color? One year you can highlight yellow, then next year, bright red. Or one year you can do all pansies, the next year, geraniums. You dare being bold because the choice isn't for forever, just for a season. Fashion trends and accessories are the same way. Take a look in your jewelry box for a glimpse of past seasonal trends. Once upon a time, I wore quite gaudy in-your-face earrings, and the more colors they had, the happier I felt. I would turn my head quickly so as to get more sparkle out of each movement. I don't wear them now, but I will not throw them away, because maybe some spring I'll feel like they again are just right, providing me the extra color and jazziness that is missing from my life or wardrobe or friends.

Annuals give that sense of individuality, that reminder that anything goes in the short-term. That parts of who we are can be replaceable. We can try it on for size, see if it fits.

Music reminds me of annuals, since I can only be a fan of any genre for a short time. I just can't seem to get anything to stick, except for a few favorites. I tire easily of any one type of music. And my own musical ability just doesn't seem to stick either.

I can sing a pretty good song, but I've tried playing the flute, the piano, the violin, and the cello, to no avail. Not that I can't squeak my way through a few songs, but a musician I am not. My partner is an excellent piano player, and he tries his best to motivate me to become skilled, especially now that I'm working on the cello. He imagines me bowing beside him, as he so expertly works his way through a tune. I also can imagine it, I just don't have the patience to practice enough to make it to a decent level of performance.

Some women are like this with careers, trying on jobs like earring styles. Out with the old, in with the new. Many of us have no choice. Through either layoffs or downsizing, our jobs are cut and we are required to re-invent ourselves. Or perhaps we become ill and suddenly are disabled in the middle of redefining who we are, what we can do, who we can become.

I quit a job once after being diagnosed with inflammatory arthritis. All I could think about was going home and going to bed, and I did that for 6 months straight. Then, one sleepless night, I decided that I was still too young to give up on work and creativity, and I began writing a children's book in my head. So instead of tossing and turning, I created a character and gave birth to my first book, "Impatient Pamela Calls 9-1-1." By morning she had a voice, a look and a cockiness that I thought would work. Today that book is on its fifth printing after winning the National Parenting Seal of Approval. Various Impatient Pamela books have been translated into four languages.

Sometimes when we try something on, it is part of life's grand adventure to see how it feels and what will come of this new, unexplored part of ourselves, and other times it leads nowhere except as a footnote to our adventures.

Maybe I'll try the drums.

# Wildflowers

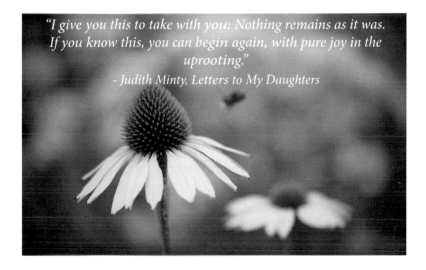

"I give you this to take with you: Nothing remains as it was.
If you know this, you can begin again, with pure joy in the
uprooting."
- Judith Minty, Letters to My Daughters

What could be more spirited than a wildflower? Their seeds
travel on the breeze, land where they may, and become produc-
tive and beautiful be it hillside or roadside. Don't mistake them
for weeds – they are exactly where they want to be, for as long as
they want to be there.

I have a little secret jealousy of women like that. They are of two ilks: Either they have total confidence in their wanderlust and it is a temporary stage in their life, or they are permanent wanderers but still looking as though they are living life to the fullest from an outsider's perspective. They can add beauty and color to the barest of scenes. They have very few needs and travel light. They might move from town to town with reckless abandon, or they might settle down for quite some time, enjoying the views around them, before moving on.

When it is a temporary stage, life can be grand. Often early in life, students will become the vagabond type and travel to foreign lands or make the most of educational experiences that allow them to blow with the wind. Or women with certain careers can do this – journalists, doctors and nurses, photographers who follow the work. My father was like this but not by choice. He had to follow the work of construction to feed his wife and seven children. So off we would go to a new town, with my mother chattering about what color she would paint our bedrooms, I think in the hopes that we would all stay positive about a new move.

Having changed schools 12 times before the 9th grade comes with a price! There is no point, for example, in making friends or getting strongly entrenched in a community because we will be moving soon. So you rely on family for those long-term connections that friends usually provide.

Yet that love of wanderlust is deep within my heart. I take that adage "the grass is always greener" to mean that life can be improved if you just move. My life has become one of resisting that urge, because as they say, "wherever you go, there you are." You bring yourself and all your baggage with you. In some ways I am glad that I married young because my then-husband, who never wanted to move anywhere, kept me grounded. And now, my partner is firmly planted on this farm where we live and has no intention of moving anywhere. His roots are planted deep. So I get my wanderlust needs met with travel.

Sometimes wandering is a choice and sometimes it is not. If you are not choosing that life, it can be lonely indeed. Perhaps the wanderlust is a temporary stage, brought on by boredom or not having any permanent roots. Eventually these women find where they will land and add their beauty to the landscape. Or, they could be running from experiences or people who just could not be tolerated. Abused or neglected women are often careful not to get too settled, lest they need to pick up and travel again, redefining themselves and their lives, though no wish of their own, or because of a need to stay protected.

I hope that your wanderlust is by choice, and that you enjoy each and every place you land. And if it is not by choice, I hope that you can settle comfortably with new people and new surroundings, adding a wealth of experiences as you go through this stage, however long it must last.

# Shrubs

"If you are a queen and I am a queen
then who will fill the bucket of water?"
– *Folk saying*

Shrubs anchor the world. There they are at the edge of the house, adding a little greenery, a little color. A cherry sage has flowers as delicate and showy as an annual. Shrubs can be as beautiful and deadly as the oleander, or as helpful as the rosemary bush growing in the Southwest. Take that same rosemary to the North, and you have a small but sturdy perennial. Shrubs are like that.

Some shrubs have poisonous foliage that sicken children and pets yet bear flowers helpful to bees, such as the Mexican Buckeye. Complicated, these innocent anchors we splash around our yards. The most flexible of plants, they will even take on another shape if you prune them into hedges, or statues, or anything that you desire. They provide the backbone of wonderful smells that we equate with spring, like lilacs of the Midwest. You don't even have to see them to enjoy their message of a new season that has arrived.

I feel badly sometimes for unappreciated shrubs. Our unsung heroes, welcoming in spring, give us flowers and sometimes fruit. They ask nothing in return, and even happily take on the shapes and the anchor requirements we ask of them. Some women are like this – the volunteers of our community, the people who take on tasks without complaint, becoming what the community requires. Those who are mothers and wives take on these roles as well, sometimes with serious pruning. Need someone to head the committee for feeding hungry families over the weekend when school lunches are not provided? Give a shrub a call.

I think it is easier to be this person once your children leave home, or if you're a career woman, once your work responsibilities diminish. You have the time and energy to devote to causes that make themselves known to you.

Even if you don't have a passion for such work now, it may come to you when your life is more settled, and you can become that anchor to which the community turns. After all, President Jimmy Carter's mother, Lillian Gordy Carter, joined the Peace Corps when she was 68. She went to India, teaching villagers about birth control, working with lepers, and giving her own life new meaning. Here is what she wrote to her children after her return:

> "I didn't dream that in this remote corner of the world, so far away from the people and material things that I had always considered so necessary, I would discover what life is really all about, sharing yourself with others — and accepting their love for you is the most precious gift of all."

This isn't my natural inclination, I must say. It is inspiring to read such accounts, but there is no way I can run off for a year or two. My world is too small for entertaining such a change. But there is much to do locally. I can have the community help define my shape, trim me back here and there for their needs. Theater is a passion of mine, so I am a board member on a local theater board, and another civic organization could use my help now, so I'll be joining them soon. We can all find ways to serve, depending on our family situations, career plans and demands, even if it is a small commitment of our time and talents.

Are you a business person? You could volunteer for the Small Business Association's SCORE mentoring program. Do you work at Walmart? You can volunteer for various non-profit organizations in your community and be recognized by their Volunteerism Always Pays (VAP) grant. I like to remind myself that although time is scarce, I have as much time in a day as the President of the United States!

Be a shrub! Anchor the world!

# *Herbs*

"How wonderful it is that nobody need wait a single moment before starting to improve the world."
– Anne Frank

Herbs are useful plants; they are the workhorses that come back year after year without complaint, and contribute to our foods for flavoring, provide us medicine, or just smell wonderful. Sometimes the leafy green parts are the most useful, and other times it's the seeds, or the bark, or the roots or even the fruits of the plant like the chive flowers. Herbs are used in different cultures for spiritual ceremonies and practices, such as the Native American practice of burning certain types of sages for cleansing ceremonies.

My herb garden is up and going this year – and it is the best one ever! Many herbs grew back from last year, so my investment was minimal as I replaced a few lost plants (some rosemary and a parsley plant), but otherwise the survivors from last year are numerous: thyme, lemon thyme; the pizza staples of oregano and chives; the soup necessities of marjoram and sage. Some I know nothing about, such as chocolate mint. What are you supposed to do with chocolate mint, anyway? But I couldn't resist it when I went shopping last year at the plant nursery.

We have a great nursery near my home called "Grass Roots" and they have an entire building dedicated to herbs. You walk in and the place smells like you should start chopping onions and get busy making a stew. How can you go wrong at such a place? I adore every plant that I bring home, and sometimes just one type of parsley isn't enough and I end up with three varieties.

Herbs are sturdy, determined plants, and they almost always survive even the cold Minnesota winters. They are beyond helpful when trying to do some good old-fashioned home cooking. Look in the fancy cookbooks these days and you'll notice they often decorate their dishes with some fresh-cut herbs. Herbs can even lift your spirits when you touch their leaves and smell your fingers.

When we think of the medicinal uses for herbs, much has been lost. The pharmaceutical shelves seem so much more efficient and safe, yet our ancestors used many plants to make soothing balms, teas and potions to help cure the sick. St. John's wort, for example, is said to lift the spirits. How our ancestors ever figured out the uses for plant extracts is beyond me, but imagine our world without aspirin. Hippocrates, seen by some as the father of modern medicine, left written records describing willow tree bark (active ingredient - salicylic acid!) and how using that powder as a medicine helped headaches and fevers – this from about 400 B.C.!

One of my most difficult times was after my husband left me after 38 years of marriage for a woman 20 years younger, and it felt as though my life had become a cliché. Even now, many years later, the toughest time is Christmas Day, because after 38 years of a Christmas Eve tradition of family, Finnish saunas, lasagna, Christmas Eve church services and opening of gifts, anything else seems empty. Then Christmas Day we would all go to my sister-in-law's home, dressed in our new sweats, and we would have a great meal and play games all day.

One horrible consequence of divorce is that you end up divorced from an entire family, not just your ex. My ex's sisters were like my own sisters when I was a young woman. They supported me as I raised my children, they embraced me into their family, which was very different from mine, and they encouraged me in my journey of pursuing an education and, later, as a career

33

woman. Even though I still talk with some of those women who had become my sisters, the days of Christmas traditions are over. Why does divorce mean that we no longer get to have people in our lives who were our relatives? It should not have to be that way.

I wanted to keep custody of my sister-in-law Ruthie after my divorce, and we have stayed in touch – much to my delight. During the winter of my divorce, she and my own sisters came to my rescue. They are the ones I call when I'm feeling low. They soothe and calm and talk me through problems, and soon, without realizing why, the problem is less and I feel better. Just like drinking a cup of chamomile tea.

Do you have that healing ability? Our counselors of this world tend to have that skill, as do many social workers, nurses, clergy, and even the very best of our doctors. Listening is part of that skill, but healing is more than listening because many people who are good listeners are not necessarily herbs. It's also that ability to help us put things in perspective, or come up with solutions, or see our lives from a broader point of view. We walk away more whole and more healed than we were before. My doctor opened her business with the name "Cup of Coffee Clinic" with that very mission – to listen and take good care.

You can develop that skill during your lifetime by becoming an active listener. When I first heard that term, it seemed silly to me because I wondered what other kind of listening there was.

It turns out there are several types, and active listening is what we do when we truly pay attention to what a person is saying. It is listening not only to their particular words, but listening to try and understand their intent, and letting them know what we understand them to be saying by paraphrasing what they are saying. That way, we can check to see if we are "getting their story." A helpful way to do this is to ask a question about what you are hearing in the conversation, such as: "Are you saying that you want me to . . . not do your laundry? . . . do less of the cooking? . . . take more free time for myself?" OK, that was wishful thinking, but you get the idea.

Even if we are not natural herbs, we can learn to be better friends, better spouses, better parents and better co-workers if we pay attention. To the herb garden to make some tea, and perhaps I'll call a sister!

# *Noxious Weeds*

"Hatred is like a poison
which you inject into your
veins, before injecting it into
your enemy."
– *Gems of Buddhist Wisdom*

Noxious weeds have no place in a healthy plant and animal eco-system. They can become invasive and take over a natural habitat for wildlife or natural vegetation. Not to mention, some are downright poisonous when burned, like poison ivy. An example in my area is the Grecian foxglove, a tall perennial. Gardeners spread the plant because it is beautiful, prolific and reproduces easily from seed. It can hybridize with garden foxglove (not poisonous!) in some areas, but it has not done so yet in Minnesota.

The Grecian foxglove is poisonous to humans, livestock and wildlife. For example, if it gets bundled in a hay bale, it can be fatal. And those flowers look so harmless!

Have you ever been a noxious weed? Poisoned some relationship or someone's reputation on purpose? I have. I remember the day when I told a rumor that would purposely hurt another, and I even remember the moment of deciding when to do this obnoxious experiment. I wondered, "Would anyone care or notice this rumor?" So I went about spinning my yarn of lies. "Did you know that Julie Minor is pregnant?" I said to one fellow seventh-grader. Then I told one more person, and I sat back and waited. (I changed her name here so as not to start yet another rumor, although she never was "PG" as they said in those days, at least not that I knew!)

I've often wondered why I did this and I have no good excuse except that my older sisters were talking about rumors, and my mother said how horrible it was to start one, and so there you have it. I had no animosity toward my unsuspecting victim – I didn't even know her very well, and she was in the 11th grade at the time. Other people had started rumors, and I just became curious about the whole process. What happens when you start one? Does anyone find out who started the rumor?

It didn't take long for me to get an answer. About two hours later, Julie Minor found me as I was coming out of the bathroom stall of the girls' restroom. How did she know I was there? Her Private Eye skills must have been keen or her people were out to protect her, because she came storming into that restroom in a fit of rage! She grabbed me by the shoulders, just like they do in movies, and gave me a firm shake. "WHY are you saying that I'm PREGNANT?" She spat in my face. Actually it was too simplistic to explain. I really just wanted to see how this whole rumor thing worked, but I couldn't tell her that. "I thought you were!" I said meekly, as though adding a lie onto my rumor behavior wouldn't make any difference.

She looked at me with dagger eyes. "I am NOT PG!! And if you ever say anything like that again, I'll knock your socks off!" She gave me one more shake, turned and stomped out.

My thoughts ranged from relief that she didn't punch me to being totally guilty for doing a bad thing to amazement that she came to me so quickly after I got that rumor ball rolling. It couldn't have been more than two hours tops. So my life as a noxious weed was shortlived. Not that I don't have a litany of behaviors to be guilty about, or a list of deeds that need forgiveness, but noxious weeds set up a certain poison, then wait to see what happens – just like I did with Julie Minor.

Noxious weeds make an environment less hospitable, less habitable (whether a school, playground, workplace or home) and they do it on purpose. They enjoy misery around them, sort of like hiding the life boat preservers and watching the panic ensue when the ship starts to go down.

At work I have seen this behavior with saboteurs. You have a good plan, you present it to some committee or work group, and the saboteur has great reasons why your idea can't work, or why the problem is too big to be solved, or how they've tried that before and there's no point in taking that kind of risk. They have practice at this, and they know that if they ask enough deep questions, no one will ever solve the problem or get to the work of the committee. The weed's poison has spread!

If you have those tendencies, it is never too late to stop. You can stop spreading rumors, lies or even innuendo about people around you. You can be a positive force for solving problems at work. We can change these behaviors by supporting others and by supporting their ideas with kindness and openness – or even neutrality if that is an easier way to start.

It isn't as easy as Thumper – remember him from the movie "Bambi" when he said "if you can't say something nice, don't say nothing at all." That's a childish phrase and its used at a childish level.

You can change noxious weed tendencies but only with intent. It has to be purposeful change. The Jewish religion says that if you stand by and hear someone being unfairly judged, and you do not speak up, you are as guilty as the speaker. Although not Jewish, I try and remember that moral code when someone is being bad-mouthed and he or she isn't present for self-defense. Use words like "In his defense . . ." or "If she were here, I bet she'd be able to explain . . ." In this case, practice helps and soon it becomes a way of thinking.

Resist the urge to be a noxious weed. Resist the urge to spread more poison in the world and decide to become a positive force for change. It's one thing to have healthy debate about issues and topics of the day to help sharpen your views and challenge your critical thinking skills; it's quite another to poison the world with rumors, gossip and half-truths. Refuse to participate!

# Trees

"Listen to the trees talking in their sleep,' she whispered, as he lifted her to the ground. 'What nice dreams they must have!'"
– L.M. Montgomery, *Anne of Green Gables*

Trees are those mighty structures that always remind me of home.

Although only part of our complex ecosystem, they are comparable to our parents, giving us comfort on a hot day, shelter in a storm, fruit for that moment when we need something sweet, wood for a home, roots to anchor our soils, food and shelter for small creatures, the beginnings of rainforest bounty and leaves to scrub the carbon dioxide out of the air. This last task has become one of their most important, with increased levels of carbon dioxide that we humans have deposited into our atmosphere. Trees are the fixers and healers of our world, just as we hope to be as parents and grandparents. Appropriately, young trees do more carbon-cleansing than the old ones, yet the old ones carry the majesty and glory that is inspiring.

Trees add so much to our lives, as obvious and oft-quoted classics such as *The Giving Tree* by Shel Silverstein shows us. Who can read that book and not think of their wish for such a giving, nurturing, sacrificing friend or parent, while still recognizing that the gifts given were too much to trade? If you haven't read it, the tree gives up first her apples, then her branches and finally her trunk for a boy in exchange for his friendship and love. The apples are for money, her branches are for him to build a house, and the trunk is because he wants to build a boat to go traveling.

I recently visited Fort Clatsop, where Lewis and Clark wintered during 1805, and I felt embraced and sheltered by the forest there, surrounded by the Columbia River and the Lewis and Clark National Historical Park. The pines speak their own language, and they grow with their own survival and purposes in mind. Survival of their species is the goal of all botany.

My children have grown up to be very independent adults, raising their own families and surrounded by their own friends, children, jobs, responsibilities and lives. There are times that I stand like that Giving Tree, wondering if their attention will ever return to me. Of course they would come if called. Still, I'm reminded about a quote I once read, that a man described himself as the "salt and pepper at the Thanksgiving table." In other words, he wasn't first and foremost in his children's or grandchildren's lives – just a bit of flavoring that rounded out a celebration.

Yet isn't that the result of successful parenting? I remind myself of that truth. Hopefully you are that sound tree that your children or grandchildren can return to when needed, yet you haven't become the victim that the Giving Tree became; giving all her apples, chopping off all her branches, finally giving up her trunk for the boy's boat needs. Yes, he had needs, as do our children and grandchildren, but one must survive that giving.

There is such a thing as too much sacrifice. Of course we would give our own lives if theirs were on the line – most parents would gladly trade their lives for that of their child, or even that of their child's pain, if given the chance. But most of the time spent while raising children is getting through the day, keeping some sense of rhythm and order while trying to teach important lessons along the way. And, of course, trying to do as little harm as possible.

It can feel lonely when they've grown up and you have that empty nest in your branches, but if you've done your job properly, they are living their lives. They smile at memories, think positively about what kind of shelter you've offered, and they'll do the same for the next generation. They'll even call you now and then, or invite you into their lives from time to time.

I enjoy singing my grandchildren songs, telling them stories, and providing the salt and pepper. This very night I am staying at my son's home, and after the nightly ritual of playing games and brushing teeth and getting drinks of water, I sang songs while rubbing backs and feet. I hope that as these grandchildren become adults, they will sometime smile and say, "My grandmother used to sing me songs when she tucked me in." What more is there?

Yet, I can't make them the purpose of my entire existence. I still need my own life, friends, passions and interests. I need to know that to not give up my entire trunk is OK. My children seem to agree, since they have no need of a boat. Thank goodness!

# *Perennials*

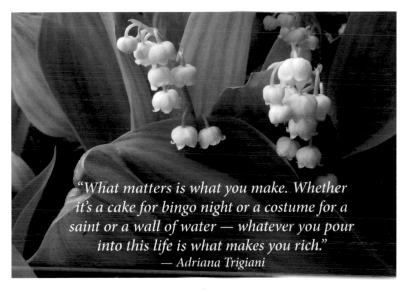

*"What matters is what you make. Whether it's a cake for bingo night or a costume for a saint or a wall of water — whatever you pour into this life is what makes you rich."*
— *Adriana Trigiani*

Perennials have such a wide range of characteristics, they are hard to describe. But one thing is true about them all – they multiply! These are the generous and prolific women who can write 20 books in their lifetime, or raise a brood of children, or manage 48 employees. Everywhere they turn, there is a time of plenty. A cornucopia, if you will, of people or projects or love depending on their focus.

There are times in our life when production comes easy – whether it's at work or at play. And it seems to come without competition. Pregnant with twins a third time? Another department to manage? Your response to either of these scenarios shows your reaction to perennial production. Could be "Yikes" or "Why not?"

My sisters gave me a hosta plant as a housewarming gift several years ago, and it was one of the rarer varieties – solid-color green leaves, tall and bushy when in full force, and gorgeous purple blooms. I've now split it into five clumps and put two of them in Duluth at my vacation rental home so that others can appreciate this fine plant.

There have been times in my life when I could add tasks with reckless abandon and not even pause to think about it. There was the semester when I studied for and then sat for the CPA exam, commuted an hour one-way to take two masters-level business courses at night, worked about half-time, and raised two small children basically by myself, which was the expectation of women at that time. Once I remember coming home with groceries on a Tuesday, putting the necessary items in the refrigerator, and looking up from studying on a Thursday to see the rest of the grocery bags still sitting on the counter. Such is the obsession of production.

If our relationships are not at the center of such production, they can fall by the wayside in our quest to get that degree, earn that promotion, or just stay busy out of a gnawing need that something is missing in our modern lives.

The pace of everything has increased, and it's hard to see where reasonableness should enter into our calendars. We also tend to keep our children so busy that they wouldn't recognize free play time if they had some.

Perennials can look like they take that all in stride, but if you don't nurture yourself in the process of production, you may find the base of your plant withering over time. Don't let that happen! Take the time to take stock, put your life in perspective and examine your priorities. Did my over-production lead to the end of my marriage after 38 years? I don't think so, because although I was running a college at the time, my children were grown and my ex needed a different type of spouse. And since he was a workaholic from a very young age, I mostly busied myself in widening my life as a distraction, waiting for him to show up. But over time those distractions became my passions.

I'm not sorry that I was as driven by career and interests as I have been. I have had an interesting and challenging life as an educator, writer, mother, wife, sister and traveler. Now I am living on a farm with my life partner, and, among other things, I am an online accounting teacher, a grandmother of six, a writer of fiction and nonfiction books, a business consultant, a business owner, a gardener, a kayaker, a director of plays, and an actress. I couldn't handle all of these roles now if I had not done so as a younger woman, because even now I can sense my life getting smaller, not larger. So the pace is manageable.

But I do wish that I had spent more time with my children and my grandchildren. We have great relationships going, but I can never get back some of the games or events that I could have attended, some of the long talks we could have had, and some of the hugs I was too busy to give. Yes, that is a regret.

So, if you are a perennial, take pause. Produce, yes, but with an eye toward obtaining a full garden that complements your personal and professional life, and that provides you with rich and varied experiences.

# Fruits and Vegetables

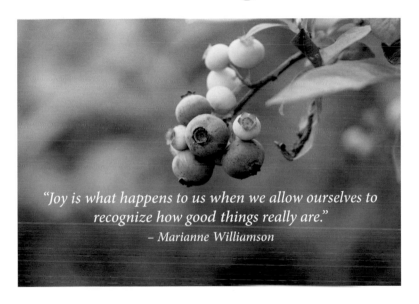

"Joy is what happens to us when we allow ourselves to recognize how good things really are."
– *Marianne Williamson*

Entire books are written about all of our plant categories, but none more so than the growing of fruits and vegetables. The wide array of available plants is staggering; their characteristics are endlessly varied; the gifts they contribute to our nutritional needs are necessary not only to sustain our bodies, but to bring joy to our hearts. There is nothing to compare to the delight of biting into a fresh, crisp apple, a ripe pear, or a juicy tomato.

The nutrients we get from these plants are so important that lack of them in the human diet can cause disease or even death. Our history books are filled with examples of explorations gone awry because of the lack of nutrients. Sailors died of rickets; camps of explorers starved.

Our ancestors learned early how to preserve not only meats, but also fruits and vegetables to save for famine times. Oh, my grandmother's canned peaches were such a special treat when I was a child, and nothing in my modern experience compares with my memories of their sweet juiciness. Maybe it is just because grandma made them.

I think of this kind of person as someone who is in the moment. Just like the joys of the produce aisle, they enjoy the serving of the day. Sort of a Buddhist sustenance combined with joy. Dare I eat a peach? These people say 'Yes!'

I expect that I can be difficult because I have high expectations of those around me. I once had a good friend tell me that I expect too much. It is true – honesty, integrity, good conversation, and a sense of privacy are all characteristics I value. And of my students, you can add critical thinking skills, seemingly neither joyous nor in the moment. Not everyone can meet those expectations all the time. So being my friend or family member or student can be difficult. I just don't hand over a joyous experience.

I have a friend from days gone by, Deb, who is an example of a joy-spreading person. She loves willingly and openly, she is funny and clever, she is caring and her counseling profession is a natural fit for her: She is a joy to be around. She'll cheer you up with what seems like no effort on her part. You can go to her house for dinner, play games afterward, have good conversation, watch a movie, and you'll leave feeling good about yourself. All this she does in an honest, open way – nothing contrived or forced, which I sometimes feel that I do.

We all need the sustenance of joy in our lives. Do you know this kind of joy-spreading woman? If so, hang on tight to that friendship! They can give you the nourishment to last you a lifetime. I now conscientiously decide that high expectations aren't always my job. Those expectations remain with my relationships with students, but I try to emulate Deb when I'm with my children and grandchildren. I relax, enjoy the moment, and take part in whatever glorious experience is going on. This afternoon my family might be going to a children's movie. Time for joy! I hope you can feel the same and spread a little bit of that openness with your family and friends.

Let life's juice drip down your chin.

# Grapes

*"An over-indulgence of anything, even something as pure as water, can intoxicate."*
– Criss Jami

Ah, grapes. The grape vines in my garden are old, and if you listened to the way my partner tells it, they must be 40 or so years old. They still produce fabulous fruit that I harvest every fall, and this year the plant was so abundant that I gave away many grapes for others to do with what they wish, be it jam, jelly or my favorite, homemade grape wine.

The life of the party, that is what they are! Even the birds are delirious with enjoyment when fall comes, and they imbibe happily then flop on the ground until they recover their flying skills after eating those fermented little pellets of wine.

Maybe it is the French in me that thinks wine is the essence of all that civilization has to offer – great combinations of food, friends, ambiance, atmosphere, uplifting conversations and lasting memories. You see it in television shows and movies, someone making a toast to all that life has to offer.

To coin a cliché, my own mother was the "life of the party," and she took that role seriously because of her Irish heritage (maiden name, Kennedy – no doubt about that one!) and her basically cheerful and delightful personality. She had ancestors from both Northern Ireland and the County of Cork, so her pedigree earned her the right to kiss the Blarney stone. She finally managed to travel to Ireland to kiss that stone during the last decade of her life. She also was an excellent cook – an ability that helped her a great deal when she was extending invitations to a dinner party. Everyone accepted! Tonight as I draft this chapter, I'm actually sipping Irish whiskey in her honor, although, quite frankly, it is too strong for my taste and I won't last long. But mother would have been able to manage it.

Are you the life of the party? Do people ask you to plan the office get-togethers because you'll know just what to serve, where to have this next great event, and who should be included? Some of us fulfill that role just because we are good planners, but most of the time we turn to the person who can handle and understand the fun of it all.

That is not me. I have to work at being involved in a social setting, and usually I have to set my mind to the task of participating in a large group. Somehow the size of the group can be overwhelming. But in my own home, I do enjoy hosting small dinner parties or, even better, barbeques. I'll even pore through cookbooks to get just the right menu, then cook all day, pretending I'm Julia Child. So, I have that bit of my mother in me.

This cooking and entertaining interest is new to me. While raising children I got quite sick of cooking and taking care of other people's stomachs. Once my children were grown and gone, I think three years went by before I cooked a single thing!

Yet social skills are needed at gatherings, and those who have these skills can go far. Just make sure you don't get too carried away by the life of the grape. It can turn on you, to be sure. One too many and not only are you not the life of the party, but you are the problem someone must solve. In the best case scenario, we must find you a driver. In the worst case, you will have to live with the results of your behavior in the memories of your colleagues and friends for the rest of your life. Lampshade jokes notwithstanding, you are no longer fun or funny. That happened to my mother at the end of her life, when after three detox experiences, our family was left with very few choices. Finally, one of my brave sisters took my mother in, and refused to let her drink in her home. My mother had a last year of sobriety and returned to her clever yet fun-loving self.

Do you have some addiction that is out of control in your life? In our modern society the list is endless – not just the familiar drug addiction, but sex, gambling, food, internet addictions, even the old-fashioned workaholics. There is an addiction out there for everyone, just waiting to suck out the energy of your life. I'm reminded of this expression, "If you don't like who you are, change your mind." Behavioral scientists aside, it can't possibly be as easy as changing your mind, but making decisions about who you will be can help you reach out for the proper care, and surround yourself with supportive people who will help make your changes possible.

My own weakness, aside from caffeine and any form of choco-late, is gambling. Well, that and my love of a good glass of wine. I vow to spend only a certain amount, or stay only so long if I visit a casino, but alas, my resolutions are short-lived when I'm sitting at machines, which are now available to most Americans less than an hour's drive away. I started my journey down this road through research for a book, "Game Over," my first fiction piece, and I still love the thrill of a poker game or a night at the casino. I've spent way too much money in the name of research, and although I continue to try and convince myself that I can manage this grape in my glass, I know that this is a weakness that must be watched. Guarded. Monitored. No fun whatsoever.

Take care to not let those grapes take control of your soul.

# Digging in the Dirt

*"You don't have to see the whole staircase, just take the first step."*
*– Martin Luther King, Jr.*

Aren't you sad when the autumn season is over, plants are all dried up, and the time has come to put an end to the growing? The end of anything is sad – even coming to the end of a book! The good news is that winter is a time to dream about what is yet to come, what possibilities lurk under the snow and in the frozen ground. It could be anything – from the most beautiful lily to a dangerous black-rot cancer that is about to take over your grape vines. One always has to hope, which is the basic definition of either a gardener or a farmer – a person filled with the idea of hope, an optimist at heart.

Then spring comes, and it's time to dig again, perhaps move around some plants, see if they will do better with more shade, more sun, or just enjoy a change of scenery.

Our lives can be like that: times of re-evaluation, re-definition of self. We are sometimes plants that do it all, such as the glorious bamboo plant, which can be used as shelter, food, clothing, and the stalks even provide music for the soul if you hold still and listen while in the middle of a bamboo forest. But doing it all comes with a price as well, and eventually those plants die, like all living things.

Or we might be late bloomers, waiting to blossom and find our gifts, such as the century plant, or another favorite as described by Buffy Phillips, "The African violet has an infrequent bloom that is simple and delicate, but beautiful and vibrant to see, but some of us must make a true effort to observe this plant in order to share its beauty." Building our lives the way we want them takes time, patience, and effort.

After I got my inflammatory arthritis, I had a brief time of despair over all that was lost – the fun of holding hands, the possibility of never running again, even if it was a short sprint to the mailbox. I, like most people with a chronic illness, had to redefine myself. No, I couldn't be just my arthritis. I had to become a person who just also happened to have this illness. All those expressions come into play, the ones people say to try and make you feel better. "Make the most of it." "Count your blessings!" Even if you want to slap those people, they are just trying to help, and they are not to blame for this new challenge you face.

I once gave up a child for adoption. This tearing of your very heart, this rendering of a pound of flesh, this giving up of spirit and your very breath, is nothing less than life altering. There are three muscle types: skeletal, cardiac, and smooth, but none of those terms describe how you feel when your heart breaks. It was 1969, a year when many were arguing for peace, and families were being torn apart around the nation. So my internal struggle seemed small by comparison. To be pro-war, pro-peace meant divisions in families that still plague us to this day. People talk about that era with nostalgia and a sort of foggy haze, much like the drug-induced smoke that reeked from the Vietnam-era vets, but for me, it was all about loss. Loss of a child I had to give up because the sexual revolution, with the advent of birth control and the promise of free love, had promises that were too late for me.

Love and sexual promiscuity came with a cost for me. I was too small-town for the consequences to be of brightness and ringing of freedom and dancing at moonlight. No, that type of freedom never came to me. Instead, my having unprotected sex resulted in a child whom I gave up for adoption in that famous year, 1969. Then, in 1995 I finally had the courage to do a search and

69

I found my birth daughter, and I now say, "Hooray!" Truth is the ultimate freedom. A daughter, and then a granddaughter, what could be more wonderful?

Redefinition of self starts with acknowledgement of who we are. If disease or past circumstances mean you have to redefine yourself, the work is yours. You are the one who must take the risks, get a different career (or be content without one) change your diet or lifestyle, face your past, fully aware that your spouse or partner may leave you. Even your children might judge you. Once you face those choices, what happens next might not be as bad as you imagine. That is what happened to me. Yes, my spouse left me for someone 20 years younger. No, I could no longer play racquetball or dream of joining the marines. No more dairy or beef or pork. (I now am to the point where I can cheat on the beef and have it a few times a year, and then of course there is that cream that magically manages to show up in my coffee!)

But here are the "yeses." Yes, I can still work and teach and travel and write, now that my arthritis is calmer and more manageable. Yes, I now have a new blending of my family. Yes, I can still hold a grandchild or play in a park, or take a grandchild college shopping, or swim in Lake Superior. I can love again after being left for another. I can make new family connections with my partner's children and grandchildren. If someone in my family rejects my love or my choices, I can move on.
And I can dig in the dirt, as can you. You can dig and plant and

transplant until the garden of your life fits who you are and what you can do. Until the plants reflect the beauty that is you, and the goals you have for yourself.

You can enjoy each stage of your life, and be ready to move on to the next gardening season, the next change, even if it is a hurricane a'comin'. Gardening teaches you that patience is indeed a virtue, just like that expression of old. When we look around and all we see is a horticultural slum, we can either dig in and make a difference, or decide it is fine for now, for this season, for this stage of our lives. And spring will come again, with a chance to renew with vigor and all the power nature has to give us.

Live in your new spring, and dig in the dirt.

# *Other works by this author*

### *Children's works, written as Mary Koski*

> #### *Impatient Pamela Calls 9-1-1*
> Winner, National Parenting Center's Seal of Approval

> #### *Impatient Pamela Says, Learn How to Call 9-1-1 (workbook)*

> #### *Impatient Pamela Asks, "Why Are My Feet So Huge?"*
> Winner, Children's Choices 2000

> #### *Color, Color, Where Are You, Color?*
> A wonderful, appealing visual treat – Midwest Book Review

### *Works for adults, written as Bernie DuBois*

> #### *Game Over*
> Filled with DuBois' perfect blend of facts, accurate detail, and fascinating characters, this story reveals the life and struggle of those with gambling problems. Crime, politics, romance, and addiction fill the lives of Debbie Wood and Craig Two Horses. A woman pitted against incredible odds, yet struggling to overcome her problem and take care of her children. A Native American man needing to find his role in his tribe and the issues of tribal sovereignty. Both are intriguing, rich stories that collide in the modern-day casino.